Til Death Do Us Part

Understanding and Keeping
Your Wedding Vows

LATONYA STERLING

Til Death Do Us Part
Understanding and Keeping Your Wedding Vows
By Latonya Sterling

Copyright © 2025 Latonya LSimmons Sterling
All rights reserved.

No part of this book may be reproduced, stored in a retrieval system, or transmitted in any form or by any means—electronic, mechanical, photocopying, recording, or otherwise—without the prior written permission of the publisher, except in the case of brief quotations embodied in critical articles or reviews.

Unless otherwise noted, all Scripture quotations are taken from the *Holy Bible, New International Version*®, NIV®. Copyright ©1973, 1978, 1984, 2011 by Biblica, Inc.™ Used by permission. All rights reserved worldwide.

ISBN: 9798999589743

First Edition

Cover design generated ChatGPT

Published by Latonya LSimmons Sterling

Contact: latonyasterling@gmail.com

Printed in the United States of America

Table of Contents

Introduction	1
Chapter 1 – What Marriage Really Means	3
Chapter 2 – I Take You To Be My	9
Chapter 3 – To Have and To Hold	15
Chapter 4 – For Better or For Worse	19
Chapter 5 – For Richer or For Poorer	23
Chapter 6 – In Sickness and in Health	27
Chapter 7 – To Love and To Cherish	31
Chapter 8 – Till Death Do Us Part	35
Chapter 9 – When Vows Are Broken	39
Chapter 10 – Hope for Struggling Marriages	43
Chapter 11 – When Divorce Happens	47
Chapter 12 – Wisdom for Singles	53
Chapter 13 – Two Become One, The Divine Design of Husbands and Wives	61
Conclusion – A Call to Covenant Love	69
Acknowledgments	73
Author's Note	75

Dedication

To my husband Marlon Sterling,
Through every season, every joy, and every challenge,
you have been my partner, my friend, and my safe place.
We have faced trials and triumphs, tears and laughter,
but I would choose you again and again.

Thank you for loving me, for walking beside me, and for
making our vows more than words spoken at an altar.
They have been the rhythm of our life together.
This book is as much your story as it is mine.

With all my love,

Latonya

Preface: The Wedding Vows

Most traditional Christian wedding ceremonies include vows similar to these:

I, [name], take you, [name], to be my wedded husband/wife,
to have and to hold from this day forward,
for better, for worse,
for richer, for poorer,
in sickness and in health,
to love and to cherish,
till death do us part,
according to God's holy ordinance;
and thereto I pledge you my faith [or] pledge myself to you.

Brief History

The wording of these vows trace back to the Book of Common Prayer (1549), compiled under the direction of Thomas Cranmer for the Church of England. For centuries, these words have shaped how millions understand marriage — as a sacred, lifelong covenant spoken before God and community of witnesses. Over time, denominations and cultures have adapted the phrasing, but the heart has remained the same: a holy promise meant to be lived out for a lifetime.

Introduction

Marriage is one of the most sacred commitments a person can make, and yet it is often one of the least understood. I remember the conversation my husband and I had with our pastor, at the time, before our wedding day. He asked if there was anything special we wanted him to include in the ceremony. Without hesitation, we asked him to take a few moments to explain the vows.

So often, brides and grooms stand at the altar filled with excitement. The wedding day has been planned for months, if not years—money spent, details chosen, dresses fitted, flowers arranged. The day is beautiful and memorable. But, once the cake is eaten, the music fades, and the honeymoon ends, the vows remain. Those vows are not just words — they are commitments that must be lived out every single day.

Before my husband ever proposed, I told him plainly. *"If I get married, it is for keeps. If divorce is an option for you, then I am not the one you want to marry."* Now, more than 20 years later, I can say with confidence that I have never regretted my decision to marry him nor to keep my vows. That doesn't mean the journey has been easy. Marriage requires cooperative work, grace, and forgiveness. But, it also brings joy, growth, and a deeper expression of love than I ever imagined.

As you read this book, I want you to know my heart. I am not writing these words to present "my way" as the only way, nor do I want anyone to feel judged or condemned by what I share. Every marriage is unique, and only you and your spouse truly know the dynamics of what happens behind closed doors. What I offer here are lessons, encouragement, and biblical insights that have helped me in my own marriage. My prayer is that some of these truths may be helpful to you as well — but ultimately, each couple must seek God's wisdom for themselves. You will read this repeatedly as a reminder throughout this book.

This book was birthed from my desire to help couples not only remember the words they said at the altar but also learn how to walk them out in real life. I'm not coming from the perspective that my marriage is perfect and that I have arrived. There is still growth needed even after 20 years. Through the lens of Scripture, through my own experiences, and with encouragement for both the strong and the struggling, I pray this book helps you see marriage not as a burden, but as a blessing — a covenant worth keeping.

Chapter 1
What Marriage Really Means

Marriage is one of the oldest institutions in human history. Long before governments created paperwork and licenses, long before civil laws defined requirements, marriage was designed by God. At its core, marriage is not a contract but a covenant — a sacred bond between one man and one woman, witnessed by God, and built to reflect His love and faithfulness. A contract is an agreement based on terms, conditions, and mutual benefit — something that can be amended, broken, or dissolved when one party fails to uphold their part. A covenant, however, is far deeper. It is a binding commitment rooted in trust, sacrifice, and unwavering devotion — not built on performance but on promise. Marriage, therefore, was never meant to function like a contract that expires or is negotiated when convenience changes. It was designed by God as a covenant — a lifelong union sealed by His presence, shaped by His character, and intended to reflect His enduring love.

The Biblical Foundation of Marriage

The very first marriage is recorded in Genesis 2. After forming Adam, God said, "It is not good that the man should be alone; I will make him a helper fit for him" (Genesis 2:18). He then fashioned Eve from Adam's rib and brought her to him. Adam's response was immediate joy: "This is now bone of my bones and flesh of my flesh" (Genesis 2:23). Scripture concludes, "Therefore a man shall leave his father and mother and be joined to his wife, and they shall become one flesh"(Genesis 2:24). This is God's design: one flesh, joined together, not just physically but emotionally, spiritually, and in covenant. Marriage is a picture of unity, companionship, and shared life under God's blessing.

The apostle Paul later expanded this understanding, teaching that marriage is meant to mirror the relationship between Christ and His church (Ephesians 5:25–32). Husbands are called to love their wives as Christ loved the church — sacrificially, faithfully, and unconditionally. Wives are called to respect and honor their husbands as the church honors Christ. Together, this creates a union that reflects God's covenant love to the world.

A Historical Perspective

While God designed marriage, cultures throughout history developed their own ways of recognizing and regulating it. In early societies, marriages were often family or community arrangements and did not require government approval. The covenant was sacred in itself.

Centuries later, governments began requiring marriage licenses and civil registration. In England, *Hardwicke's Marriage Act of 1753* established strict legal requirements to prevent clandestine or invalid unions. The *Marriage Act of 1836* in England then allowed non-religious (civil) marriages, shaping the legal, not just religious, recognition of marriage.

In the United States, marriage licenses became common in the 19th century as states sought to regulate marriages, track vital statistics, and, in some eras, enforce unjust racial restrictions. Over time, licenses became the legal proof of a union, even though the biblical covenant always preceded paperwork.

Today, birth, marriage, and death certificates are part of civil registration systems used for population records and legal rights. These systems help society function, but they are not the true foundation of marriage. The covenant before God remains primary.

Why does this matter? It's easy to get caught up in cultural or legal definitions of marriage. But, marriage is not simply about paperwork, ceremonies, or tax benefits. At its heart, marriage is about two people committing their lives to one another before God, promising to love, honor, and remain faithful in every season. This means marriage is not disposable. It is not a convenience to be set aside when things get difficult. It is a covenant designed to last a lifetime, empowered by God's grace.

Every Marriage is Unique

While the biblical foundation is unchanging, every marriage is unique. No two couples share the exact same story. That's why it's so important to seek God personally for your marriage. Advice and books, including this one, can help, but they are not a substitute for His voice. I encourage you to walk closely with God as you navigate your marriage.

Reflection: Building on God's Design

Encouragement Thought
Marriage is God's idea. It is more than a legal document — it is a sacred covenant meant to reflect His faithful love.

Scripture Anchor
"Therefore what God has joined together, let no one separate."
(Mark 10:9)

Prayer
"Lord, thank You for creating marriage. Teach me to see it as You do — a holy covenant, not just a human contract. Help me and my spouse to build our marriage on Your foundation, seeking You daily as we live out our vows. In Jesus' name, amen."

Journal Prompts

- When I think about marriage, do I see it more as a covenant or a contract? Why?
- What does it mean to me personally that marriage reflects Christ and the church?

- How does knowing the history of civil records help me separate God's design from man's systems?
- What areas of my marriage (or preparation) do I need to place more intentionally in God's hands?

Latonya Sterling

Chapter 2
I Take You to Be My...

When we stand before God and speak the words *"I take you to be my..."*, we are declaring something sacred and deliberate. Those words are not merely ceremonial; they are a covenantal declaration of *intentional* choice and wholehearted commitment. To *take* someone in marriage is not to possess them, but to purposefully receive them—to open your heart and your life to walk together in unity, faith, and purpose.

The word *take* itself carries power. It is active, not passive. It means, *"I am choosing you on purpose."* It is a conscious acceptance that says, *"I see who you are—your strengths, your flaws, your dreams, and your humanity, and I choose to walk with you."* That moment of taking is not about emotion; it is about covenant. It is a decision that carries the weight of devotion, honor, and endurance. In a world where people are often taken for granted, taken advantage of, or taken lightly, there is something profoundly sacred when two people stand before God and each other and say, *"I take you"*—and mean it.

From the very beginning, we see this intentional reception in Scripture. When God brought Eve to Adam, he didn't stumble into affection—he recognized her as the one designed to walk with him. Genesis 2:23 says, "This is now bone of my bones and flesh of my flesh; she shall be called Woman, for she was taken out of Man." Adam's declaration was not born from impulse but revelation. He saw her and received her as a gift meant for companionship and shared purpose. That same sense of recognition should mark every marriage. I'm not saying that God has assigned one person to another, but that each partner intentionally acknowledges the sacredness of who they are choosing to walk beside.

The story of Jacob and Rachel beautifully illustrates this truth. In Genesis 29, Jacob met Rachel and loved her with determination. He worked seven years for her father, Laban, so that he could marry her, and Scripture says those years "seemed like only a few days to him because of his love for her." That kind of devotion reveals that Jacob's choice was rooted in commitment, not convenience. When Laban deceived him and gave him Leah instead, Jacob did not abandon his purpose—he worked another seven years for Rachel, the woman he had chosen. Fourteen years of labor demonstrated a heart that valued love as a covenant worth waiting and working for.

Jacob's story reminds us that love is not a feeling that one falls into; it is a decision one stands in. It is endurance, perseverance, and steadfastness. When Jacob finally took Rachel as his wife, it was the fulfillment of years of labor and unwavering desire—a love proven by consistency. That is the weight of *"I take you"*—to choose, not once, but continually, through every season. We are not saying, *"I take ownership of you."* We are saying, *"I receive the opportunity to love, serve, and grow with you."*

Marriage is a divine partnership—a place where two people intentionally join their lives to reflect God's love and character to one another and to the world. It is a relationship designed for transformation, for refining the heart, and for learning the depth of grace. This kind of love mirrors the way Christ loves the Church. Ephesians 5:25 says, "Husbands, love your wives, just as Christ loved the church and gave himself up for her." (NIV) Christ's love was not accidental or emotional—it was intentional, sacrificial, and anchored in purpose. That same mindset shapes a healthy marriage. Each partner chooses daily to receive, honor, and love the other—not because they feel like it, but because they vowed to.

To *take* your spouse is to step into covenant, not contract. A contract says, "I'll stay as long as this benefits me." A covenant says, "I'll stay because I vowed to." Covenant love is not dependent on performance but grounded in promise. It endures when emotions waver, when circumstances shift, and when life tests its foundation.

When we truly take our spouse, we are declaring that we will keep receiving them—again and again—as life changes. We receive them in joy and in struggle, in health and in hardship, in growth and in weakness. It is a continual choice to say, *"I take you still."*

That is the beauty and the weight of those words. *"I take you"* is not a one-time declaration—it's a daily decision. It's a reflection of steadfast love, of purpose joined with faith, and of two lives intentionally intertwined to reflect God's covenant love to the world.

Reflection: Choosing with Intention

Encouragement Thought
Saying *"I take you to be my…"* is not a phrase of emotion but of intention. It is a sacred choice to receive another person as your lifelong partner in purpose, growth, and reflection of God's love. To *take* someone is to say, "I see you, I choose you, and I will keep choosing you."

Scripture Anchor
"This is now bone of my bones and flesh of my flesh; she shall be called Woman, for she was taken out of Man." (Genesis 2:23)

Prayer
"Lord, thank You for the gift of covenant love. Teach me to love with intention — not out of emotion, but out of commitment and faith. Help me to see my spouse as the one I have chosen and continue to choose, reflecting Your steadfast love in our union. May our marriage honor You and draw us both closer to Your heart. In Jesus' name, amen."

Journal Prompts
- What does *taking* my spouse mean to me personally?
- How can I practice choosing my spouse intentionally each day?

- What can I learn from Jacob's commitment to Rachel about endurance and faithfulness in love?
- In what ways can I better reflect God's steadfast love in how I receive and love my spouse?

Latonya Sterling

Chapter 3
To Have and To Hold

When you stood at the altar and said *"to have and to hold,"* you were speaking words of deep commitment—words that reach far beyond romance or a physical embrace. To *have* someone means to receive them fully as a gift from God. To *hold* someone means to cherish, protect, and remain close, even when life is difficult.

A Biblical Foundation

In Genesis 2:24 we read: "That is why a man leaves his father and mother and is united to his wife, and they become one flesh." Some translations say the man will *"hold fast"* to his wife. That phrase carries the sense of clinging tightly, not letting go, remaining steadfast.

Marriage was never meant to be casual or distant. It is a covenant of closeness. To hold one another is not only about physical touch but about being present—heart to heart, soul to soul. "To have and to hold" also speaks of intimacy. This is not limited to the physical union, though that is a beautiful and important part of marriage. It also means emotional intimacy—listening, sharing, encouraging, and walking through life together.

One of the greatest gifts of marriage is companionship. Ecclesiastes 4:9–10 says, "Two are better than one, because they have a good return for their labor: If either of them falls down, one can help the other up." God did not design marriage for distance but for togetherness.

Holding in Real Life

When my husband and I first said our vows, I thought I understood what it meant to "hold" one another. But, over the years, I've learned that holding is not just about closeness in the easy times. It's about standing together when everything around you feels like it's falling apart.

For us, holding each other has not always meant quiet forgiveness or long, emotional conversations. It has meant learning to humble ourselves enough to speak the words, *"I'm sorry,"* even when it wasn't easy. It has meant recognizing when to talk and when to wait, allowing space for the right moment instead of forcing resolution. Holding has also meant being prayerful—for one another and with one another—especially during difficult times when neither of us had the right words. Sometimes support looked less like physical closeness and more like spiritual covering. But what holding looks like in my marriage may not be what it looks like in yours. That is why it's important to ask God what it means for your marriage to be marked by this vow. Every couple has a different rhythm, different strengths, and different struggles. Holding your spouse might look like encouraging them in their dreams, praying over them in weakness, or simply staying by their side when life gets heavy.

Reflection: What "Holding" Looks Like in Your Marriage

Encouragement Thought
To "have and to hold" is not a one-time action spoken at the altar—it is a lifelong posture of closeness, loyalty, and care. It means choosing one another every day, even when it's inconvenient or uncomfortable.

Scripture Anchor
"Above all, love each other deeply, because love covers over a multitude of sins." (1 Peter 4:8)

Prayer
"Lord, thank You for giving me the gift of my spouse. Teach me what it means to truly hold them—not only in moments of joy, but also in times of weakness and struggle. Show us how to walk in deeper intimacy and unity, with You at the center. In Jesus' name, amen."

Journal Prompts
- What does "to have and to hold" mean to me personally?
- In what ways do I feel most held by my spouse?
- In what ways can I be more intentional about holding my spouse's heart and not just their hand?
- What is one small step I can take this week to grow our intimacy and companionship?

Latonya Sterling

Chapter 4
For Better, For Worse

When a couple stands at the altar, *"for better, for worse"* sounds noble and romantic. It is easy to say when life is good, when the dress fits perfectly, when family and friends are smiling, and when love feels effortless. But, these words are not just for the sunshine—they are for the storms.

A Biblical Foundation

Jesus said in Matthew 7:24–25, "Therefore everyone who hears these words of mine and puts them into practice is like a wise man who built his house on the rock. The rain came down, the streams rose, and the winds blew and beat against that house; yet it did not fall, because it had its foundation on the rock." Within marriage you will experience rain, streams, and winds. The vow *"for better, for worse"* acknowledges that life will not always be easy. The strength of your marriage is not found in the absence of storms, but in your shared foundation on Christ.

Every marriage will have seasons of joy. The "better" moments might be the birth of children, the fulfillment of dreams, financial blessings, or simply the delight of laughter shared in quiet evenings at home. These times remind us of the goodness of God and the joy of companionship. It is important to treasure these moments. Too often we overlook the good seasons while bracing for the next challenge. Part of living the vow means choosing gratitude, thanking God for the blessings and celebrating your spouse in the good times.

The "worse" moments are often the ones that test the vow. They may be financial strain, health struggles, miscommunication, disappointments, or even betrayal. These times can make you feel like giving up. But, they can also become the very seasons where your marriage grows roots that cannot be shaken. I remember teaching my daughters to think carefully about marriage. I told them, *"Before you say 'I do,' think about the worst thing someone could ever do to you. Could you forgive? If not, don't get married."* Because *for better or for worse* is not just poetic language—it's real life. Every marriage will face both sides of that promise.

We can never predict what "worse" will look like. It may not be betrayal or tragedy; sometimes it's simply growing pains, disappointment, or unmet expectations. What feels small to one couple can feel unbearable to another. The point isn't to expect something terrible—but to prepare your heart for the reality that you will be tested in marriage. Marriage requires forgiveness, grace, and humility long after the vows are spoken.

For my husband and me, there have been moments when "worse" pressed us beyond what we thought we could bear. At times it felt like everything was pulling us apart. But, by God's grace, we learned that "worse" does not have to mean the end—it can mean a new beginning. Thank God for the mature married couples in our lives who coached us along the way that our marriage would yield success.

Still, every marriage is different. Again, what feels unbearable to one couple may be a challenge another couple easily navigates. That is why you must seek God for how to walk through your own valleys. He alone knows the weight of your burdens and the strength of your covenant.

When you said *"for better, for worse,"* you weren't promising that life would always be easy. You were promising your spouse that they would not face it alone. Marriage means standing side by side through both the sunshine and the storm clouds.

It doesn't mean you'll never stumble. It doesn't mean you'll never cry. It means you choose, again and again, to walk hand in hand, trusting that God's grace is enough for both of you.

Reflection: Finding God's Presence in Your Unique Seasons

Encouragement Thought

The vow *"for better, for worse"* is not about perfection—it is about presence. It is about being there for each other when life brings joy, and being there still when it brings pain. God never promised a storm-free life, but He promised His presence in every season.

Scripture Anchor
"The Lord is close to the brokenhearted and saves those who are crushed in spirit." (Psalm 34:18)

Prayer
"Lord, thank You for being near in every season of life. Help us to treasure the better times with gratitude and endure the worse times with faith. Teach us to lean on You and on one another when life feels overwhelming. Give us grace to stand together, no matter what comes. In Jesus' name, amen."

Journal Prompts
- What has been one of the sweetest "better" seasons in our marriage, and how did it strengthen us?
- What has been one of the most difficult "worse" seasons, and what did we learn from it?
- How can we better support each other when challenges arise?
- In this current season, what is one way we can draw closer to God and to each other?

Chapter 5
For Richer, For Poorer

When we hear the words *"for richer, for poorer,"* it is easy to think in extremes. Many imagine either living in abundance or struggling in poverty. But, in reality, finances in marriage are much more complex than just the amount of money you have.

A Biblical Foundation

The Bible reminds us that God is the ultimate provider. Philippians 4:19 says, "And my God will meet all your needs according to the riches of his glory in Christ Jesus." This doesn't mean we will always live in wealth, but it does mean God is faithful to supply what we need.

Marriage requires couples to trust God for provision, but it also requires good stewardship of what He provides. Proverbs 27:23 says, "Be sure you know the condition of your flocks, give careful attention to your herds." In today's terms, that means paying attention to your finances, planning wisely, and caring for what God has entrusted to you.

In our marriage, my husband and I never lacked. We always had enough—and often more than enough to bless others. But, that didn't mean finances were easy for us. Our challenge wasn't about whether we had money—it was about how we handled it.

My husband has always been more of a spender, while I am more of a saver. He wanted to enjoy the blessings of life, while I wanted to preserve and prepare for the future. For him, my tight grip on the budget sometimes made him feel poor, even though we had plenty. For me, his spending felt risky, even when we could afford it.

It took us years to learn that financial stewardship isn't about one personality winning over the other. It's about finding balance—budgeting in a way that allows for preservation *and* enjoyment, security *and* generosity.

"For richer, for poorer" also prepares us for seasons we don't see coming. What happens when one spouse loses a job? What happens if the household depends on two incomes, and suddenly one is gone? These are the kinds of trials that can strain even strong marriages. In those moments, couples must return to the foundation: God is still the provider, and marriage is still a partnership. Blame, fear, and resentment can easily creep in, but this is the time to come together rather than pull apart.

I remember when I gave birth to our first son. My husband and I agreed that we didn't want to deal with daycares because of the constant exposure and uncertainty. So, he told me that I could stay home, and together we would figure it out. At first, I kept my job but reduced my hours to less than part-time so that we could adjust gradually. By the time our son, Marcel, turned three, I made the decision to come home fully. My husband made sure we were in a stable position financially so that I could do so—and even made it possible for us to enroll Marcel in private school, despite his own spending habits. That season reminded me that "for richer, for poorer" isn't about how much money comes in; it's about how much unity and trust exist when circumstances shift. Adjustments may be necessary—downsizing, reprioritizing, or tightening the budget—but the strength of the covenant is never measured by the size of the paycheck. It is measured by a shared commitment to keep God first and to stand together through every season.

Ultimately, financial stewardship in marriage is about unity. Amos 3:3 asks, "Do two walk together unless they have agreed to do so?" Couples must agree on how to manage what they've been given. That doesn't mean you will always see eye to eye, but it does mean you commit to working toward agreement. Budgeting is not punishment—it is a plan. It allows couples to allocate resources in a way that honors God, provides for the home, and makes room for joy and generosity.

Reflection: Trusting God as Provider in Your Story

Encouragement Thought

Money will test a marriage—not only when it is scarce, but even when it is abundant. Stewardship is not about how much you have, but how faithfully you manage what you've been given together. The vow *"for richer, for poorer"* is a reminder that God is the source, and marriage is the partnership.

Scripture Anchor
"Two are better than one, because they have a good return for their labor: if either of them falls down, one can help the other up." (Ecclesiastes 4:9–10)

Prayer
"Lord, thank You for providing for our needs. Teach us to be good stewards of all You've entrusted to us. Help us to find balance in how we view and manage money, so that we walk together in unity. In seasons of abundance and in seasons of lack, remind us that You are our provider. Amen."

Journal Prompts
- Are we more naturally spenders, savers, or somewhere in between? How has that shaped our marriage?
- How can we create a budget that reflects both preservation and enjoyment?
- If we suddenly faced a financial loss, how could we support one another instead of turning against one another?
- In what ways can we use our finances to not only provide for our family but also bless others?

Chapter 6
In Sickness and In Health

When we promise *"in sickness and in health,"* we acknowledge that our love will not only endure the vibrant, healthy days, but also the seasons of weakness, pain, and limitation. Marriage is not just about sharing joy—it is about carrying one another through struggle.

A Biblical Foundation

The apostle Paul reminds us in Galatians 6:2, "Carry each other's burdens, and in this way you will fulfill the law of Christ." That principle applies deeply to marriage. In times of sickness, weakness, or weariness, we are called to carry the weight together with practical help. Ecclesiastes 4:10 echoes this truth: "If either of them falls down, one can help the other up. But pity anyone who falls and has no one to help them up." Marriage gives us a partner to lean on, someone who will be present and supportive when life knocks us down.

"In sickness and in health" certainly includes physical illness, but it also extends further. Sometimes sickness is not in the body but in the mind or emotions. Depression, anxiety, or burnout can affect one spouse and weigh on the marriage. In those moments, the healthy partner becomes a source of encouragement, patience, and prayer. Likewise, even in seasons of health, we need one another. Life-altering events, like childbirth or recovery from trauma, require care and support.

Sometimes being "in health" doesn't mean we don't need help—it means we are strong enough to give it.

In my own marriage, we have seen this vow lived out in both directions. When I delivered both of my sons by C-section, my husband was there every day, taking care of me in every way—including bathing me when I could not move easily. Later, after a fire in 2021, I developed sciatica and bursitis in my hips that left me down for weeks. My husband never once treated me like a burden. He made sure I ate, drove me to every appointment, and even made a pallet in the back of our truck so I could lie down when sitting was too painful. He never complained. He simply helped.

I have had the privilege of standing by my husband through his surgeries—rotator cuff surgeries, gallbladder removal, and even an unexpected quadruple bypass. For nearly two months, our family room became our bedroom as I cared for him around the clock. It was my pleasure, not my burden, to make sure he had every comfort, every meal, and every bit of love he needed. Each time, he expressed gratitude, often with tears, but I knew this was not just duty—it was covenant.

I have also witnessed this vow lived out faithfully in others. There is a sister in my ministry whose husband doesn't fully walk. I have watched her lovingly stand by him without hesitation. When he was first injured, she ran to him—she didn't throw him away because he could no longer walk. As a matter a fact, she was away at sea. She left her job on the ship to care for him fulltime. Her love became a visible testimony of commitment. Another sister in the ministry was hospitalized for an extended period, and her husband, a pastor, cared for her faithfully. Though he still had to work, running his own business, he was never too tired to make sure she was cared for. All the while, he trusted God continually for her healing. Finally, I watched my mother tirelessly care for my father, even while battling her own health challenges, as he fought pancreatic cancer until the day he passed away. Through their love and devotion, I have seen living examples of what it truly means to honor God, their vows, and their spouses in sickness. It is not just admirable—it is possible.

This vow calls us to a love that does not flinch at weakness. It requires patience when recovery is slow, compassion when suffering is great, and humility when roles are reversed. It means remembering that health is not guaranteed, but love can remain steady.

Every couple's journey with sickness and health will look different. Some may face chronic illness, others may experience only occasional setbacks. The important thing is not to compare stories but to ask: How is God calling us to live this vow in our marriage?

Reflection: Learning Compassion in Your Marriage

Encouragement Thought
Sickness has a way of testing couples—but it also has a way of bringing them closer. Caring for one another in weakness reflects the love of Christ, who bore our burdens and carried

our pain. When you serve your spouse in moments of need, you are not only loving them, you are honoring God.

Scripture Anchor
"Be kind and compassionate to one another, forgiving each other, just as in Christ God forgave you."(Ephesians 4:32)

Prayer
"Lord, thank You for the gift of health, and thank You for the grace to endure seasons of weakness. Teach us to care for each other with compassion and patience. Help us not to see illness as an interruption of love, but as an opportunity to deepen it. In every season—whether in strength or in weakness—may we reflect Your love to one another. In Jesus' name, amen."

Journal Prompts
- When I think of the vow *"in sickness and in health,"* what memories come to mind from our own marriage?
- How has caring for one another in weakness deepened our bond?
- Where do I need to grow in patience or compassion when my spouse is not at their best?
- How can we prepare our hearts and home to walk faithfully through future seasons of sickness or limitation?

Chapter 7
To Love and To Cherish

When a bride and groom say *"to love and to cherish,"* they are not merely promising warm feelings or temporary emotions. Love in marriage is not about butterflies in the stomach or the glow of romance—it is a covenant commitment. Love is active and constant.

God Is Love

The Bible does not just say that God loves; it says that *"God is love"* (1 John 4:8). That means love is not something He switches on and off. It is who He is. When we say we love our spouse, we are committing to treat them with the same character and consistency with which God loves us. 1 Corinthians 13 describes this love: "Love is patient, love is kind. It does not envy, it does not boast, it is not proud. It does not dishonor others, it is not self-seeking, it is not easily angered, it keeps no record of wrongs. Love does not delight in evil but rejoices with the truth. It always protects, always trusts, always hopes, always perseveres." (vv. 4–7).

This is not about sentiment. It is about action. It is a decision to love with patience when your spouse is short-tempered. To love with kindness when you feel misunderstood. To forgive when your heart wants to hold on to offense. But, let's be honest: this is not easy. We are human. Feelings get hurt. Words get spoken that shouldn't be. There are days when demonstrating love feels natural and effortless, and there are days when it feels costly.

Loving your spouse does not mean you never struggle. It means you acknowledge those struggles, repent when you fail, and choose forgiveness when you are wronged. Marriage requires a constant rhythm of repentance and forgiveness—both giving and receiving. Real love is not pretending everything is perfect; it is working through imperfections together.

Cherishing goes a step further. To cherish means to treat as precious, to honor, to protect, and to hold in high regard. It is more than simply coexisting. It is actively valuing your spouse. Cherishing looks like speaking words that affirm rather than tear down, noticing the small things your spouse does and expressing gratitude, and choosing to see your spouse through the lens of their worth in Christ rather than focusing only on their weaknesses. It means making time for connection, even in busy seasons, and protecting your spouse's heart by being trustworthy and faithful. When you cherish someone, you are saying, "You are not replaceable. You matter to me. I will treasure who you are, not just what you do."

Love and cherish are not easy vows, but they are life-giving. When practiced, they create a marriage where both husband and wife feel secure, valued, and deeply loved. And even when one partner struggles, God's love can supply what we lack.

Reflection: Asking God What Cherishing Looks Like

Encouragement Thought
Love is not a feeling—it is a covenantal choice to reflect God's character in marriage. Cherishing is the daily expression of that love in practical ways. Even when feelings waver, God's Spirit enables us to keep loving and to keep cherishing.

Scripture Anchor
"Be devoted to one another in love. Honor one another above yourselves." (Romans 12:10)

Prayer
"Lord, thank You for showing us what love looks like through Your Son. Teach me to love my spouse with patience, kindness, and forgiveness. Help me to cherish them, to see their worth through Your eyes, and to treat them as a precious gift. Give us both the humility to repent quickly and the grace to forgive freely. Amen."

Journal Prompts
- When I think of God's love for me, how does it challenge the way I love my spouse?
- In what ways can I show my spouse that I cherish them this week?
- Where do I need to practice repentance in my marriage?

- Where do I need to extend forgiveness?
- How can we create daily rhythms that remind each other, "You are precious to me"?

Chapter 8
Til Death Do Us Part

Of all the vows spoken at the altar, *"till death do us part"* may be the most sobering. It is a declaration that this covenant is meant to last a lifetime. In a world where relationships are often treated as temporary or conditional, this vow reminds us that marriage is not built on convenience. It is built on covenant.

A Biblical Foundation

In Mark 10:9, Jesus said, "Therefore what God has joined together, let no one separate." Marriage is not simply two people making a decision—it is God joining two lives into one. That union is meant to endure until death parts us. The "no one" also includes the individuals within the marriage.

The apostle Paul compares marriage to the relationship between Christ and the church (Ephesians 5:25–32). Christ's love for His bride is unbreakable, steadfast, and sacrificial. Our marriages are called to reflect that same enduring love.

In today's culture, commitment is often treated lightly. Many see marriage as disposable—something to leave behind when it no longer feels fulfilling. But, biblical marriage is different. It is not built on shifting emotions or circumstances; but should be anchored in the decision to remain faithful.

That does not mean marriage is without struggles. Feelings change. Life brings pressure. Personalities clash.

Seasons shift. But, the vow *"till death do us part"* is a reminder that marriage is not about holding on only when it is easy. It is about choosing to stay when it is hard.

There are moments in some long marriages when one or both spouses wonder if they can keep going. Sometimes those moments are brief, and sometimes they feel overwhelming. But, perseverance is not about never struggling—it is about choosing covenant love in the middle of the struggle. This vow also gives stability. Knowing that divorce is not an option allows couples to focus on reconciliation, healing, and growth rather than escape. It creates a sense of safety— *"I am not leaving, no matter what comes."*

When my husband and I were dating, I told him from the beginning that divorce was not an option for me. I made that decision long before marriage because I had watched my unsaved parents endure many difficult years together, even through turmoil. If they could hold on without Christ, I believed my marriage could endure even more with Christ at the center. I told my husband that if he was going to marry me, death was his only way out. A friend once asked if I thought that kind of commitment might give him the freedom to cheat. I laughed and said, "No. Imagine being stuck in a covenant relationship with someone you don't want to be with!" In my mind, his only other option was to value me and our marriage so that he wouldn't have to live in misery until one of us died. It's something to laugh about now, but I meant it then—and I still mean it.

That mindset shaped how I viewed our covenant. It meant that every disagreement had to lead back to resolution, not resentment. It reminded us to keep communication open (though still a work in progress), because silence builds walls while conversation builds bridges. It taught us to practice forgiveness quickly so that bitterness would not take root. It encouraged us to celebrate milestones—anniversaries, victories, and even the small wins that remind us of God's grace. It also showed us the importance of community: surrounding our marriage with godly couples and wise counsel. We have wonderful married friends and pastors we can call on if needed. Most of all, it taught us that seeking God consistently is what keeps a covenant strong. A marriage built on Him has the strength to endure any storm.

Marriage is not about perfection, but about perseverance. When you said "till death do us part," you were declaring a love that lasts. And while your ability to truly walk in love will be tested, it will also be refined. Yet, sometimes circumstances beyond our control cause a marriage to end despite our best intentions. That does not make anyone a failure—God's grace still meets us there, bringing healing and new beginnings. With His help, your marriage—or your heart—can still be a testimony of enduring covenant love in a world that desperately needs to see it.

Reflection: Seeking Strength to Finish Well

Encouragement Thought
The vow *"till death do us part"* is not about chains—it is about covenant. It is about finding security in knowing that no matter what comes, you are not walking alone. With God as your anchor, perseverance is possible.

Scripture Anchor
"Let us not become weary in doing good, for at the proper time we will reap a harvest if we do not give up." (Galatians 6:9)

Prayer
"Lord, thank You for joining us together in covenant. Give us strength to remain faithful through every season of life. Teach us to forgive quickly, to love deeply, and to persevere with hope. May our marriage reflect Your unbreakable love until the day You call us home. Amen."

Journal Prompts
- When I think about the vow *"till death do us part,"* what feelings or fears come up for me?
- How can we strengthen our marriage so it not only survives but thrives long-term?
- What practices or rhythms can we put in place to remind each other that this covenant is for life?
- How do I want to be remembered by my spouse at the end of our journey together?

Chapter 9
When Vows Are Broken

When we stand before God and promise our vows, we do so with hope and sincerity. None of us imagine a day when those vows might be broken. Yet, the reality is that many marriages experience betrayal, dishonesty, neglect, or abandonment that shatter trust.

A Biblical Foundation

Scripture acknowledges the weight of broken promises. Malachi 2:14 says, "The Lord is the witness between you and the wife of your youth. You have been unfaithful to her, though she is your partner, the wife of your marriage covenant." Broken vows grieve the heart of God because they damage what He designed to be whole. But, the Bible also shows us God's heart for restoration. Psalm 34:18 reminds us, "The Lord is close to the brokenhearted and saves those who are crushed in spirit." Broken vows are not the end of God's story. His grace is still available—for the one who broke trust and for the one who was wounded.

Few things cut as deeply as betrayal in marriage. Whether it comes through infidelity, dishonesty, or neglect, broken vows create wounds that are not easily healed. Trust, once shattered, cannot be rebuilt overnight. Some couples try to push past the pain without ever addressing it, but healing requires honesty. The brokenness must be acknowledged. Repentance must take place. Forgiveness must be extended. And even then, restoration is a process that takes time.

Typically, when people think of broken vows, they immediately think of infidelity. But vows are broken in many other ways. Vows are broken when spouses dishonor one another by yelling, calling each other names, or speaking with contempt. Sometimes spouses use joking as a subtle way to insult one another—this is a form of passive aggression that wounds the heart and erodes intimacy. Husbands often think of protecting their wives from outside harm, yet sometimes forget to protect them from inner harm—the kind caused by harsh words, indifference, or neglect. Likewise, wives can dishonor their husbands by belittling them in public, withholding respect, or refusing to support their leadership.

Vows are broken when one spouse becomes emotionally unavailable, showing no interest in the other's dreams or burdens. They are broken when there is a lack of support during sickness or hardship. They are broken when selfishness replaces sacrifice, when comparison replaces contentment, or when a spouse withholds affection as punishment. Even spiritual neglect—failing to pray together, ignoring each other's spiritual growth, or refusing to forgive—can quietly violate the covenant of love that marriage represents.

In Scripture, one example of broken vows beyond infidelity can be seen in the story of Michal, the daughter of Saul and wife of David (2 Samuel 6:16–23). When David danced before the Lord in worship, Michal looked down on him with contempt. Her words dishonored her husband and revealed a heart of pride rather than partnership. Though she did not commit adultery, her disdain and disrespect broke the unity of their covenant. Her attitude created distance, showing that betrayal of the heart can occur through dishonor just as deeply as through unfaithfulness.

Forgiveness does not mean forgetting or pretending it didn't happen. It means releasing the right to revenge and allowing God to work in the heart of the offender. For the one who broke the vow, repentance means changing one's mindset to line up with truth, turning completely from the sin, humbling oneself, and committing to rebuild trust step by step.

Marriage cannot heal without both forgiveness and repentance working together. One without the other leaves the wound open. This definitely takes God to work in the heart of both spouses. Practical steps toward healing can include seeking counseling, as sometimes an outside, godly perspective is needed to walk through deep wounds. Rebuild slowly, remembering that trust is restored through consistency, not quick words. Set healthy boundaries that create accountability and help prevent further damage. Lean on community by surrounding yourself with couples who support restoration rather than gossip or division. And, above all, pray together—even broken prayers invite God's healing presence.

It's important to remember, not every couple's story will look the same. Some marriages recover from broken vows and emerge stronger. Others end despite deep effort. What matters most is seeking God for your own journey. He knows your heart, your pain, and your path forward.

Reflection: Healing Through God's Wisdom

Encouragement Thought
When vows are broken, the pain is real, but so is God's power to heal. Whether through restoration or a new chapter, His grace is enough for both the offended and the offender.

Scripture Anchor
"He heals the brokenhearted and binds up their wounds." (Psalm 147:3)

Prayer
"Lord, You see the pain of broken promises. You understand the depth of betrayal. We ask for Your healing touch over wounded hearts. Help us to forgive, and give us the courage to walk in repentance where we have failed. Restore what can be restored, and carry us with Your grace in every step. In Jesus' name, amen."

Journal Prompts
- Have we experienced moments where trust was broken in our marriage? How did we respond?
- What steps can we take to rebuild trust and move forward in a healthy way?
- Where do I need to extend forgiveness? Where do I need to seek forgiveness?
- How can we invite God more deeply into our healing process?

Chapter 10
Hope for Struggling Marriages

Every marriage, no matter how strong, will face some type of struggle. Some struggles are external—financial stress, health crises, or the demands of work and children. Others are internal such as miscommunication, unmet expectations, or differences in temperament. In those seasons, it can feel like hope is slipping away. But, struggle does not have to mean defeat. With God at the center, even weary marriages can be renewed.

A Biblical Foundation

The apostle Paul wrote, "Being confident of this, that he who began a good work in you will carry it on to completion until the day of Christ Jesus." (Philippians 1:6). The same God who began your marriage is faithful to sustain it. In Ezekiel 37, God asked the prophet, "Can these dry bones live?" From the outside, the valley looked hopeless. But, God breathed life into what was dead. In the same way, He can breathe new life into marriages that feel dry, lifeless, or beyond repair.

Sometimes what feels overwhelming in marriage is actually very common. Many couples struggle with communication breakdowns, differing expectations about money, intimacy, or roles, and the challenges that come with adjusting to new life stages such as raising children, becoming empty nesters, or entering retirement. They may also experience conflict over in-laws, family traditions, or cultural differences, all of which can place strain on their relationship if not handled with understanding and grace. These struggles are not necessarily signs that a marriage is doomed. They are signs that the marriage needs attention, grace, and intentional care.

God never designed us to do marriage in isolation. Proverbs 11:14 says, "Where there is no guidance, a people falls, but in an abundance of counselors there is safety." Counseling is not a sign of weakness—it is a tool for growth. There was a time when my husband and I faced difficulty in our marriage and decided to meet with a marriage coach. During our sessions, he emphasized two pivotal principles that can strengthen any marriage if taken to heart: keep Christ at the center, and set aside quality time to communicate with one another. Whenever we talked to him about our struggles, he would have us turn and address each other directly. That simple act reminded us that our issues weren't just topics to discuss—they were opportunities to reconnect.

Spending time with healthy, godly couples or trusted mentors can also bring perspective and encouragement. My husband and I now lead the marriage ministry at our church community, and we do something fun and strengthening for marriages every quarter. We also have a core circle of married friends outside of our church community that we spend time with once a month. This encourages and strengthens each of us individually and as couples. Being around marriages that are thriving reminds you that hope is possible and that every relationship, no matter how tested, can grow stronger when Christ remains the foundation.

Hope is not found in ignoring problems but in facing them together. It is choosing to fight for your marriage rather than against each other. It is remembering that your spouse is not your enemy, but your partner. It is also about prayer. When we invite God into our struggles, He provides wisdom, patience, and peace. Even small steps—praying together, setting aside time to talk, or showing small acts of kindness—can begin to shift the atmosphere of a marriage.

Reflection: Inviting God Into the Struggle

Encouragement Thought
Struggle is not the end of your marriage—it can be the soil where deeper love takes root. With God, there is always hope.

Scripture Anchor
"With man this is impossible, but with God all things are possible." (Matthew 19:26)

Prayer
"Lord, thank You that no marriage is beyond Your reach. Breathe life into the areas of our relationship that feel dry or broken. Teach us to see each other with compassion, to communicate with honesty, and to keep You at the center. Give us hope when we feel weary, and remind us that with You, all things are possible. Amen."

Journal Prompts
- What struggles in our marriage feel the heaviest right now?
- Which of those struggles may not be dealbreakers but opportunities for growth?
- Have we considered counseling or mentorship from a healthy married couple?
- How can we begin to invite God more intentionally into our marriage this week?

Chapter 11
When Divorce Happens

Few words carry as much weight and pain as *divorce*. When we marry, we don't stand at the altar expecting an ending—we stand believing in forever. My husband and I made a decision before marriage that we would not even joke about divorce. Yet, for many, divorce becomes a reality. This has not been my reality. I have never been divorced. My husband and I are still going strong after a little more than twenty years. So, I do not speak with authority from personal experience. However, I have walked closely beside many who have endured the pain of divorce—including my husband, who experienced it before we met. I have sat with and ministered to couples who were deeply troubled in their marriages and have witnessed both restoration and separation take place. God has allowed me to see and learn from those experiences, giving me a small degree of insight I can authentically share even though I have not lived it myself. Nevertheless, I recognize that what I share may not apply to every couple in the same way. Each marriage has its own story, and only God fully knows the depth of what two people walk through together.

A Biblical Understanding

Malachi 2:16 is often quoted: "God hates divorce." Some people interpret this as God hating divorced people or condemning them to shame. But, that is not what

Scripture teaches. God hates divorce because of what it does to His beloved children. Divorce brings pain, brokenness, and division—things God never intended for His creation. However, while God hates the effects of divorce, He does not hate those who have experienced it. His heart is for compassion, healing, and restoration. I've witnessed this personally through my husband's journey. After sixteen years of marriage and children together, his first marriage ended through a unique annulment process. He never expected his covenant to break; he wanted to fight for it. At the time of the separation he was a new believer, and his wife at that time did not yet share his faith. The unraveling of their relationship left him angry, heartbroken, and hopeless. The emotional aftermath was a storm of confusion and grief—proof that the tearing apart of a union touches every part of the soul. Yet, even in that darkness, the grace of God met him. Over time, the Lord healed his heart, restored his hope, and showed him that even after deep relational loss, redemption is possible.

Jesus addressed divorce in Matthew 19, pointing back to God's original design for marriage as a lifelong covenant. Yet even there, He acknowledged the reality of human brokenness. The Pharisees asked why Moses permitted divorce, and Jesus explained it was because of the hardness of human hearts (Matthew 19:8). In other words, divorce was never God's ideal, but it became a concession in a fallen world.

Divorce is not just a legal action—it is the tearing apart of what God joined together. That tearing is painful because marriage was designed for unity. For some, divorce follows years of betrayal, abuse, or abandonment. For others, it results from unresolved conflict, miscommunication, or simply drifting apart. Whatever the cause, divorce leaves wounds—spiritual, emotional, and relational.

It is important to say clearly, divorce does not put someone beyond God's love, grace, or redemption. Many born again believers wrestle with guilt, believing they are disqualified from God's blessings because their marriage ended. But, Romans 8:38–39 reminds us that nothing can separate us from the love of God—not even divorce.

The church must do a better job of walking alongside the divorced with compassion rather than condemnation. Divorce is not the unpardonable sin. Healing and new beginnings are possible in Christ.

For those who have gone through divorce, there is still hope. God is a restorer of broken hearts. He can heal wounds, provide strength for single parenting, and even write new stories of love and redemption in His timing. For those who are still married but struggling, understanding God's heart toward divorce can bring perspective—divorce is never His best, yet His grace does not abandon those who have experienced it. The truth is, there are circumstances that some of us have never faced and may not fully understand—such as spousal abuse, habitual infidelity, or situations where safety and emotional well-being are at risk. It's easy to say what we *think* we would do if we were in someone else's position, but when the reality becomes personal, the choices are far more complex. Only God truly knows the full story behind each broken covenant. What we can know for certain is that His compassion extends to every hurting heart, and His power to restore remains unchanged.

Divorce should never be the first option — only the last. Before you throw in the towel, give God space to work. Allow Him to heal what has been wounded, rebuild what has been weakened, and breathe life into what feels dead. I understand that some situations in marriage appear impossible, beyond human effort or logic, and God does not force His will against ours. He invites — He does not coerce. Sometimes one spouse may fight for restoration while the other refuses, and in those cases, the outcome may not look like reconciliation even when one heart longs for it. Yet I cannot ignore the testimonies I have witnessed with my own eyes: a couple who walked into court to finalize their divorce, only to walk out recommitted to love; a friend who remained separated for six years, sustained and strengthened by God, and ultimately restored to his wife. These stories do not guarantee what God must do — they reveal what God *can* do. Marriage is a covenant worth fighting for, and when two hearts yield to God, even the ashes of brokenness can become a place of beauty again. May we never give up too quickly, never close the door too soon, and never stop believing that what seems impossible to us is not impossible for Him.

Reflection: Experiencing God's Grace

Encouragement Thought
Divorce is painful, but it is not the end of God's plan for your life. His grace is big enough to cover your past, His healing is deep enough to restore your heart, and His love is strong enough to carry you into a hopeful future.

Scripture Anchor
"The Lord is close to the brokenhearted and saves those who are crushed in spirit." (Psalm 34:18)

Prayer
"Lord, Thank You that Your love never fails—even when human love does. For those who have walked through divorce, bring healing and hope. For those struggling in their marriage, bring wisdom and guidance. Help us to see Your heart—not of condemnation, but of compassion. In Jesus' name, amen.

Journal Prompts
- What emotions or beliefs do I hold when I think about divorce?
- If I have experienced divorce, how have I seen God's grace meet me in that season?
- How can I extend compassion rather than judgment to others who have gone through divorce?
- What does it mean to me personally that nothing can separate me from God's love?

Latonya Sterling

Chapter 12
Wisdom for Singles

Marriage is a gift, but it is not something to rush into or treat casually. For those who are single, the time before marriage is not wasted time. It is preparation time. This chapter is not specifically written to tell singles to prepare themselves for marriage. Rather, it's a reminder that we must allow God to help us grow simply because we are human beings. Whether single or married, our ultimate goal should be to become the best version of ourselves *for the Lord*. However, if we don't allow God to deal with things such as childhood traumas or broken relationships now, the residue of those experiences will carry over into marriage and manifest as greater challenges. Marriage has its own set of struggles, and while it's impossible to address every issue before saying "I do," it's wise to confront as much as possible beforehand.

One of the things my mentor challenged me to do was to learn how to live life without having a man in it. During that season, I made an intentional decision not to have a boyfriend. I learned to enjoy my own company, to have fun, and to spend time with my sisters in Christ. Eventually, I reached a place where I could see couples without longing for what they had. I was genuinely content being single. My mentor also encouraged me to allow God to heal any unresolved issues I had with men from my past so that when I met the man who would become my husband, even if he displayed some of the same behaviors as someone from my past, I wouldn't view him through the lens of my past pain. That lesson helped me tremendously. Even when my husband exhibits behaviors similar to those I've seen before, I don't compare him to anyone else—his mistakes are his own.

Learning to be whole in God before entering marriage doesn't make you perfect. It simply positions you to love from a place of healing rather than hurt. The choices made in singleness lay the foundation for the kind of marriage you will one day have.

A Biblical Foundation

Proverbs 18:22 says, "He who finds a wife finds what is good and receives favor from the Lord." Marriage is a blessing, but it is also a responsibility. Entering into marriage requires maturity, wisdom, and a heart surrendered to God. Paul, in 1 Corinthians 7, also reminds us that singleness has purpose. It provides undivided devotion to the Lord. This season is not about waiting idly for marriage, but about growing in Christ, discovering your calling, and becoming whole in Him.

One of the wisest steps singles can take is to build genuine friendship before stepping into romance. Friendship lays the groundwork for trust, understanding, and companionship. It allows you to see a person's character without the cloud of emotions leading the way. Couples should discuss their faith early before feelings get involved and judgment is clouded. Moreover, they need to consider how they will live out their walk with God together. These

Til Death Do Us Part

conversations don't remove all future struggles, but they prevent surprises and build unity from the start.

Marriage should not be entered into based on chemistry alone. Physical attraction fades and emotions fluctuate, but friendship endures. That doesn't mean attraction doesn't matter. I've often heard people in ministry say that looks aren't important, but sometimes we over-spiritualize and forget to be realistic. There was a time when I honestly feared that if I waited on God, He might pair me with someone I wasn't attracted to—because of the way some people in the church talked. Some people almost made it sound like there was something wrong with wanting someone to whom you were attracted. I don't know about anyone else, but I couldn't imagine being intimate with someone I didn't find attractive. Of course, I wanted a husband who knew and loved Christ, but I also wanted someone I could look at and not cringe.

I'll never forget when I was dating a man who was incredibly godly and a true gentleman, yet there was simply no spark. My mentor wisely told me, "Don't sacrifice the spark." She wasn't suggesting that attraction should be the foundation of the relationship, but that it should be *a* part of it. Her advice reminded me that while character and faith are essential, physical attraction plays a healthy role in connection and intimacy within marriage.

When love is in the air, it's easy to get swept up in excitement and overlook important conversations. But, the healthiest marriages are built on openness and agreement in the things that matter most. Before saying "I do," couples need to talk honestly about several important areas of life. If you are a born-again believer, the very first and most essential question to settle is whether the other person is saved as well. Scripture warns us, "Do not be unequally yoked with unbelievers. For what partnership has righteousness with lawlessness? Or what fellowship has light with darkness?" (2 Corinthians 6:14, ESV). Entering into marriage with spiritual unity provides a foundation for everything else that will be built together. Couples should discuss finances—whether they are spenders, savers, or opposites—and how they will budget, give, and plan for the future. Conversations about children are essential as well, including whether they both want children, how many, and how they will respond if one partner cannot have children. They should also talk about parenting styles, such as how they will discipline and what values they will instill in their children.

Clarifying roles and responsibilities is equally important—what each expects from the other in the home, at work, and in ministry. Remember that although you want Christ at the center of your relationship, all marriages will not look the same when it comes to roles and responsibilities. Your marriage won't mirror anyone else's. In some homes, the husband may take care of the outside while the wife focuses on the inside. In my household, my husband and I share those duties. We both do yardwork and housework. While I do most of the cooking, he often cleans the kitchen. What matters most is that your marriage honors God. Don't let others establish how things should function in your home. It's a covenant between you, your spouse, and God. This is not a rejection of wise counsel, especially in areas where you and your spouse may need godly input, but it is a reminder that unity and agreement within your own home are what truly matter.

A helpful resource for couples preparing for marriage is H. Norman Wright's book *So You're Getting Married*. In it, Wright encourages couples to discuss the kinds of issues most overlook—finances, children, family traditions, and conflict resolution. Books like these can help uncover blind spots and guide couples into wise conversations before the wedding day.

Marriage is not about two perfect people coming together—it is about two imperfect people committed to a covenant. The best preparation for marriage is not finding the "perfect spouse," but becoming the kind of person who can honor God within marriage. Too often, people carry around a list of what they want in a spouse. I know I did. But after a failed relationship that I thought would lead to marriage, I realized that while I thought I knew what I wanted, I definitely didn't know what I needed. Looking back, I thank God for helping me dodge the bullet of what would have been a disastrous marriage and for opening my eyes to see that my list for the "right man" was far less than what was best for me.

I started dating the man who is now my husband about 3 years after the broken relationship, and he is so much more than what I would have settled for years earlier. This isn't to insult my ex. It's simply an honest reflection of where I was at the time. I wasn't the best choice for anyone during that season, and I certainly didn't have the wisdom to choose who would be best for me. Growth and maturity taught me that preparation for marriage begins with becoming the person who can love well, forgive deeply, and reflect God's grace within the covenant.

Premarital counseling can also be invaluable. It provides a safe place to ask difficult questions, talk through expectations, and seek biblical wisdom before saying "I do." My husband and I went through a six-month premarital training course before we got married, and it was truly one of the best investments we ever made. Because the ministry we attended at the time used H. Norman Wright's manual, we learned invaluable things that couples don't usually discuss before marriage. I still remember one simple but eye-opening lesson about grocery shopping together. You'd be surprised how quickly a war can break out in the grocery store when two people have different spending habits! That course prepared us to navigate real-life situations—big and small—with understanding and grace. It helped us build on the solid foundation of Christ that led to success in communication, respect, and faith, when put into practice, before ever stepping into the covenant of marriage.

Movies, culture, and even some church circles can paint unrealistic pictures of marriage. Some expect constant romance, others expect their spouse to "complete" them. But, the truth is, only God can complete us. A spouse is a companion, not a savior. Entering marriage with realistic expectations will prevent unnecessary disappointment.

The waiting season can be challenging, but it is not wasted. Singleness is not a punishment. It is preparation. While waiting, we learn contentment, grow in maturity, and draw closer to God so that when the time for partnership comes, we are ready to love from a place of wholeness. I don't necessarily believe God handpicks a spouse for us, but He does provide wisdom and discernment to help us see clearly. When a potential relationship arise, He gives insight to recognize character, compatibility, and red flags that emotion alone might overlook. Rushing ahead often leads to regret, but seeking God's guidance brings peace and clarity. Isaiah 40:31 reminds us, "But they who wait for the Lord shall renew their strength; they shall mount up with wings like eagles; they shall run and not be weary; they shall walk and not faint." Waiting well isn't about standing still—it's about growing stronger, wiser, and more grounded in faith until we can make an informed, Spirit-led decision about who we will walk with in covenant.

Reflection: Seeking God Before the Covenant

Encouragement Thought
Marriage is not something to take lightly. It is a lifelong covenant that deserves careful preparation. Singleness is not a season of lack, but a season of growth—time to become the person God created you to be before joining your life with another.

Scripture Anchor
"Unless the Lord builds the house, the builders labor in vain." (Psalm 127:1)

Prayer

"Lord, thank You for the season of singleness. Teach me to use this time to grow in You, to discover who You have created me to be, and to prepare my heart for covenant love. Give me wisdom to ask the right questions, to have the conversations that matter, and to wait on Your timing. In Jesus' name, amen."

Journal Prompts
- What important conversations do I need to have before marriage?
- Am I being honest with myself about my financial habits, parenting expectations, and lifestyle values?
- How am I using my singleness to prepare spiritually, emotionally, and practically for marriage?
- In what ways can I trust God more fully with my future?

Chapter 13
Two Become One: The Divine Design of Husbands and Wives

Marriage is a divine partnership designed by God, not simply a social arrangement or emotional connection. From the beginning, God created man and woman to complement one another—distinct, yet united in purpose. Scripture tells us, "Therefore a man shall leave his father and his mother and hold fast to his wife, and they shall become one flesh" (Genesis 2:24, ESV). This union reflects not just companionship but cooperation—two people walking together in alignment with God's purpose.

The husband is called to love his wife "as Christ loved the church and gave himself up for her" (Ephesians 5:25, ESV). That is a tall order—one that requires humility, sacrifice, and strength rooted in grace, not ego. Too often, men are taught—especially in church settings—that their primary measure of godliness is their ability to provide materially for their families. They are frequently told, "A man who does not work should not eat," referencing 2 Thessalonians 3:10. However, that verse addresses laziness and idleness among *believers* who refused to work while relying on others—not a husband's value, masculinity, or identity. The reality is that some men cannot work due to disability, illness, or circumstances beyond their control, yet they still faithfully lead, love, and steward their homes under God's authority.

While it is true that a husband carries a responsibility toward his family, Scripture places that responsibility in the context of love and care, not just economic performance. "In the same way husbands should love their wives as their own bodies. He who loves his wife loves himself. For no one ever hated his own flesh, but nourishes and cherishes it" (Ephesians 5:28–29, ESV). The call to "nourish and cherish" speaks to holistic stewardship—emotional, spiritual, and practical care—not merely financial provision. When we don't understand the total context of a scripture, we risk pressuring men into equating their worth with income, and we create burdens that God never intended.

Another verse often taken out of context is: "If anyone does not provide for his relatives, and especially for members of his household, he has denied the faith and is worse than an unbeliever" (1 Timothy 5:8, ESV). This passage is frequently used to place all financial responsibility on husbands, but that is not its original context. In the surrounding verses, particularly verse 4, Paul explains that *children and grandchildren* are instructed to care for their widowed mothers or grandmothers. The focus is on ensuring that widows who are truly in need are cared for by their families first, rather than becoming a burden to the church. Paul even distinguishes between widows who are genuinely without support and those who still have family or means. 1 Timoth 5:8 is a broader call for all family members to take responsibility in caring for their own, especially the vulnerable.

This does not excuse a husband from caring for his household. While Scripture does not define this care strictly in financial terms, it does call husbands to take responsibility for the well-being of their families in a Christlike, sacrificial way.

When Adam was placed in the garden, *provision was already there*. God had supplied everything needed for life and sustenance before Adam took his first breath (Genesis 2:8–9). Adam's responsibility was not to *create* provision but to *steward* what God had provided. Likewise, a husband's role is to trust God as the ultimate Provider and to steward the resources, wisdom, and responsibilities entrusted to him. This is what enables a man to truly provide for his family.

There is nothing more comforting to a man than a helpmate who knows how to encourage him, pray for him, and remind him that he is not alone. Many men have been raised to hide their emotions—to be tough, stoic, and silent. Yet strength and vulnerability are not opposites. A man who feels safe enough to express his heart to his wife shows trust, not weakness.

A helpmate—or *helpmeet*—is more than a companion. She is a partner in purpose. The Hebrew word for "helper" in Genesis 2:18 is *ezer*, the same word used to describe God's help toward humanity. That means the wife's role carries divine strength. She is not beneath her husband, nor is she above him—she stands beside him. When Paul says that "the head of a wife is her husband" (1 Corinthians 11:3, ESV), this is not a call for dominance, but for divine order. Just as Christ is the head of the church, the husband is meant to lead in love, not control. A wife "covers" her husband by praying for him, interceding when he's weary, and speaking life when his confidence wavers. Her covering is spiritual, not hierarchical.

    I have personally met many women who exemplify what it means to be a godly helpmate. I remember visiting my mentor's home on Sundays and watching her with Dad Dotson. In my immaturity, I thought she was doing too much by the way she so willingly served him. But as I grew, I realized that what I had witnessed was love in action—submission from a place of strength, not weakness. She served him joyfully, without complaint, and it was one of the most beautiful demonstrations of honor I had ever seen. I have another sister in Christ who amazes me because she absolutely protects her husband's reputation. She never speaks ill of him or exposes his shortcomings to others. Instead, she covers him in prayer and trusts God to work in him before she ever involves anyone else. I also watch my pastor and how she interacts with her husband, who is the head pastor. He has an over-the-top sense of humor, but no matter what he says or does, she never publicly corrects or belittles him. She always handles him with grace. I am grateful to God to be surrounded by women like these—women who understand the beauty of submission and the power of letting God's hand be evident in their marriages. They are the type of women you cannot tear your husband down to because they will not participate in dishonor. They model what it truly means to respect, protect, and cover.

    Throughout Scripture, we find examples of women who truly complemented and strengthened their husbands. Priscilla and Aquila worked together in ministry, teaching and strengthening others in the faith; their unity allowed God to use them powerfully as a team (Acts 18:24–26). Abigail's wisdom and discernment saved her household from destruction. Though her husband Nabal acted foolishly, she demonstrated godly character that God honored (1 Samuel 25). Sarah followed Abraham's leadership in faith even when she did not fully understand God's plan, and Peter later referenced her as an example of respectful partnership (1 Peter 3:5–6). Mary and Joseph walked through uncertainty together, trusting God through unimaginable circumstances as they raised the Savior of the world (Matthew 1–2). Each of these women illustrates that being a helpmate is not passive; it's powerful. Their wisdom, faith, and humility made them indispensable partners in fulfilling God's purposes.

In today's culture, marriage has been redefined to fit personal desires rather than divine design. The world often teaches independence instead of interdependence, competition instead of cooperation, and emotional impulsivity instead of spiritual stability. Many believers unknowingly adopt these attitudes—seeking control, validation, or material gain—rather than walking in biblical love and unity. Some women place pressure on their husbands to buy things or maintain lifestyles that have nothing to do with true provision. Scripture warns us, "It is better to live in a desert land than with a quarrelsome and fretful woman" (Proverbs 21:19, ESV). A nagging spirit can destroy peace in a home, just as pride or silence can suffocate love. Others adopt the world's view of equality that denies God's design for complementary roles. In today's culture, some measure authority and worth through financial status, leading to the belief that whoever earns the higher income should lead the home. As a result, women who make more money than their husbands may be tempted to diminish his role as the head, assuming that provision equals position. But biblical headship is not assigned by paycheck—it is rooted in God's order, not economic power. A husband's role as the head of the household is based on spiritual responsibility and Christlike leadership, not salary comparison or job status. Meanwhile, some men interpret leadership as dictatorship rather than stewardship. God's design for marriage is not one person ruling over another—it's two people serving one another out of reverence for Christ (Ephesians 5:21).

When both husband and wife operate in their God-given roles, marriage becomes a living picture of Christ and His Church. (Please note that these roles have nothing to do with who cooks, cleans or takes the trash out. That is decided within individual households.) The husband leads with love, and the wife responds with honor. He sacrifices, and she supports. He prays over her, and she prays for him. Together, they become one—a unified expression of God's heart on earth. A godly marriage doesn't mean perfection—it means partnership. It means both husband and wife trusting that God's design is not outdated or oppressive but freeing and fruitful. As Ecclesiastes reminds us, "Two are better than one… For if they fall, one will lift up his fellow" (Ecclesiastes 4:9–10, ESV).

When a couple stands before God and speak their vows, these are not just words. They are entering into a divine covenant that mirrors Christ's love for the Church. The vow to love reflects the husband's charge to love sacrificially. The vow to honor reflects the wife's call to respect and support. And the vow to cherish embodies mutual care, tenderness, and spiritual covering. When both understand their roles as God intended, the vows become more than promises—they become a living testimony of two hearts joined under one Lord, walking together in purpose until death truly does part them.

Reflection: A Covenant Worth Fighting For

Encouragement Thought
Marriage is not sustained by feeling, convenience, or performance — but by covenant. When we step into God-designed roles, we don't lose ourselves; we find purpose in unity. We reflect Christ when we choose humility over pride, service over self, and partnership over independence. No marriage is perfect, but every marriage submitted to God has the potential to be strengthened, restored, and beautifully transformed.

Scripture Anchor
"Two are better than one… For if they fall, one will lift up his fellow." Ecclesiastes 4:9–10 (ESV)

Prayer

Father, thank You for the covenant of marriage — a sacred gift that reflects Your love for Your people. Teach us to love as You love, to serve as You served, and to honor one another in word, heart, and action. Where there is strain, bring healing. Where there is distance, draw near. Soften what has grown hard, restore what feels broken, and strengthen what remains. Help us walk in grace, humility, and unity, choosing covenant over convenience and commitment over comfort. May our marriage testify of Your faithfulness and bring glory to Your name. Amen.

Journal Prompts

- Where in my marriage can I be more intentional about loving, honoring, or supporting my spouse?
- What does covenant mean to me personally — and how does that truth shape the way I approach challenges?
- In what areas have I relied on personal expectation instead of God's grace, design, or order?
- What is one practical, Spirit-led way I can strengthen unity and partnership in my marriage this week?

Conclusion
A Call to Covenant Love

Marriage is not a one-day event—it is a lifelong journey. On the wedding day, vows are spoken with joy and confidence. But as the years unfold, those vows must be lived out daily … I take you, to have and to hold, for better, for worse, for richer, for poorer, in sickness and in health, to love and to cherish, till death do us part.

Each vow carries weight, not because of the words themselves, but because of the covenant behind them. They are not promises made lightly. They are commitments made before God and lived out through His grace.

For Married Couples

If you are married, I pray this book has reminded you of the beauty and the seriousness of your vows. Marriage will not always be easy. There will be days of laughter and days of tears, seasons of abundance and seasons of lack, moments of strength and moments of weakness. But, God is faithful in every season, and His love can sustain you through them all.

Do not walk your marriage journey in isolation. Surround yourselves with *godly couples*, seek wise counsel when needed, and keep Christ at the center of your covenant. Remember that your spouse is not your enemy but your partner, and together you can face whatever life brings.

For Singles

If you are single, let this be a reminder that marriage is not to be taken lightly. Take time now to grow in Christ, to know yourself, and to prepare your heart for covenant love. Don't be afraid to ask the hard questions in relationships—about finances, children, faith, and expectations. Waiting is not wasted when it's spent becoming the person God has called you to be.

A Reflection of God's Love

Ultimately, marriage is more than a human institution—it is a reflection of God's covenant love for His people. In Ephesians 5, Paul describes marriage as a picture of Christ and the church. That means every marriage has the opportunity to show the world what covenant love looks like: selfless, patient, forgiving, enduring.

A Final Word of Encouragement

Whether you are married, single, divorced, or remarried, know this: God's love is unchanging, and His grace is sufficient. He is able to heal broken places, restore what has been lost, and strengthen what feels weak.

Marriage is a covenant worth keeping. And when kept with God's help, it becomes not only a blessing to the couple but a testimony to everyone around them.

"Now these three remain: faith, hope and love. But the greatest of these is love." (1 Corinthians 13:13)

Prayer
"Lord, thank You for the gift of marriage and the beauty of covenant love. Strengthen every couple who reads this book, and prepare every single person for the covenant You have in store for them. Teach us to love as You love, to forgive as You forgive, and to walk in grace every day. May our lives and marriages reflect Your faithfulness. Amen."

Latonya Sterling

Acknowledgments

I would like to take a moment to honor the men and women of God who have played such a vital role in shaping our marriage and walking with us through different seasons of life.

To our current pastors, **James and Denise Wheeler** — Thank you for not only ministering to us, but also walking alongside us as we serve and lead in the marriage ministry. Your support and example mean more than words can say.

To **Pastors Duncan and Dolores Dotson** (Dad & Mom) — Thank you for mentoring me as a single woman and preparing my heart for marriage. The wisdom you shared laid a foundation that helped me walk into this covenant with faith and confidence. Observing you was rewarding.

To **Bishop Courtney B. McBath and Pastor Janeen McBath** — Thank you for performing our wedding ceremony and setting us on the path of covenant love with wisdom and prayer.

To **Pastor David Martin** — Thank you for teaching our premarital class and laying a strong biblical foundation before we said "I do." Thank you also for walking with us as our marriage coach during a challenging season, always reminding us of your motto: *"Keep Christ in the center."* That truth has carried us more than once and remains a guiding light in our marriage.

Latonya Sterling

To **Pastor Mark and Dawn Lawrence** — Thank you for your counsel in our marriage and for allowing us the privilege of serving in the marriage ministry. Your trust and guidance have strengthened us as both a couple and as leaders.

Each of you has sown seeds of wisdom, faith, and love into our marriage, and for that, we are deeply grateful. This book would not be what it is without your investment in our lives.

With heartfelt thanks,

Latonya Sterling

Author's Note

Thank you for taking the time to walk with me through these pages. Writing this book has been more than just words on paper. It has been a journey of remembering my own vows, reflecting on God's faithfulness in my marriage, and being reminded of the grace that carries us through both the joys and the challenges.

I don't claim to have all the answers. Every marriage is different, and every couple has their own story. My hope is not that you would follow my way, but that you would seek God's way for your marriage. If something you've read here has encouraged you, challenged you, or given you a new perspective, I pray you take it to Him and let Him guide your steps.

Marriage is not always easy, but it is worth it. It is a covenant that reflects the love of Christ for His church, and it is one of the most beautiful gifts God has given us. Whether you are married, single, divorced, or preparing for marriage, I want you to know that God sees you, He loves you, and He has a plan for your life that is greater than you can imagine.

I pray this book leaves you with hope, encouragement, and a renewed commitment to love as God loves.

With gratitude and grace,
Latonya Sterling

Word's From a Husband's Heart

Many of us have spent years watching television portray what it believes love looks like. I'll be the first to admit—I'm a Hallmark girl. My husband and I enjoy watching those movies together, listening to beautifully scripted words that make romance feel effortless and poetic. But that's television. Real life doesn't always give us language like that.

While this book was still being written, I encountered words, on Facebook, that stopped me in my tracks. I don't doubt that there are strong, loving marriages all around us, but it is rare to encounter such thoughtful, vulnerable, and poetic expressions written by a real husband about his real wife. This wasn't a screenplay or a polished script created for an audience. It was a man publicly opening his heart and articulating the beauty, mystery, and sacred design of marriage as he lives it.

What moved me most was the tenderness and intentionality behind his words. A man being this openly expressive about his love for his wife is powerful—beautiful and sacred.

With the author's gracious permission, I am honored to share this tribute with you. My prayer is that it blesses your heart as deeply as it blessed mine, and that it encourages, challenges, and reminds us all what love can look like when it is spoken and lived with care, humility, and wonder—revealing God's design for marriage in all its breathtaking beauty.

From Dr. Taehyun Lee to Mayonaise Cabansag Lee

Marriage norms are one of the foundational parts of the Creation Mandate, deeply rooted as a default in natural law. It is more than just two different individuals being united as one. It is two worlds colliding and merging into a new breed and another level of adventure and blessings.

Every day is a discovery of mysteries of my world merging your world, allowing your world to invade mine, striving to transform each other's worlds into something much better and bigger according to God's original creational design of perfect goodness, with a great hope to witness heavenly and godly outcomes produced during the process. Every day, I see the biblical design reflected/mirrored in my marriage just as the Scripture describes how the new heaven will eventually merge the new earth, forming the new Jerusalem, a completely restored paradise of God's presence and reign.

This post may sound very philosophical or abstract. But marriage has brought me incomprehensible happiness and blessings that make me mesmerized and awestruck by God's mastermind behind it.

Baby, it is still a mystery to me, but it is true to say "Happy wife, happy family." Happy 2nd Church Wedding anniversary! I love you more today than yesterday!

Works Cited

The Holy Bible, English Standard Version. Crossway Bibles, 2001. Scripture quotations are taken from this translation unless otherwise noted.

Evans, Jimmy. *Marriage on the Rock.* Gateway Press, 1994.

Wright, H. Norman. *So You're Getting Married.* Harvest House Publishers, 1999.

Chapman, Gary. *The Five Love Languages: How to Express Heartfelt Commitment to Your Mate.* Northfield Publishing, 1992.

Eggerichs, Emerson. *Love and Respect: The Love She Most Desires; The Respect He Desperately Needs.* Thomas Nelson, 2004.

"Hardwicke's Marriage Act 1753." *The National Archives,* www.nationalarchives.gov.uk. Accessed 6 Oct. 2025.

"Marriage Act 1836." *UK Government Legislation Archive,* www.legislation.gov.uk. Accessed 6 Oct. 2025.

"History of Civil Registration in the United States." *National Center for Health Statistics,* Centers for Disease Control and Prevention, www.cdc.gov/nchs/us-registration.htm. Accessed 6 Oct. 2025.

Suggested Readings

Jimmy Evans – *Marriage on the Rock*
A powerful resource that teaches biblical principles for building a strong, unshakable marriage.

H. Norman Wright – *So You're Getting Married*
A practical guide that helps couples prepare for marriage by having important conversations before saying "I do."

Emerson Eggerichs – *Love & Respect*
It opened my eyes to how men and women often see love differently and why respect matters so much to a husband.

Previous Works

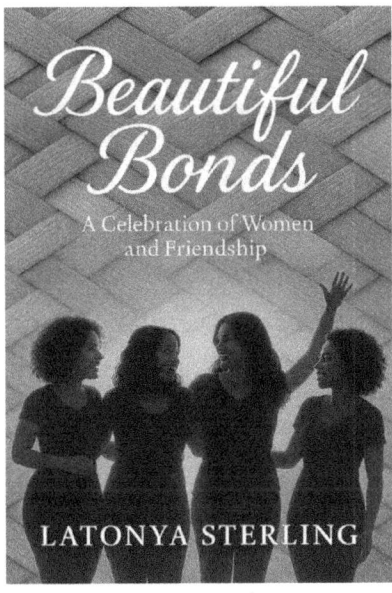

COMING SOON

Frustration: When Expectations Don't Match Reality explores the tension between what we hope for and what unfolds. It reveals how unmet expectations can lead to disappointment yet also become opportunities for growth and faith. This book offers encouragement to trust God's and find peace when life doesn't go as planned.

www.ingramcontent.com/pod-product-compliance
Lightning Source LLC
Chambersburg PA
CBHW061459040426
42450CB00008B/1421